Engineering Marvels

Stand-Out Skyscrapers

Area

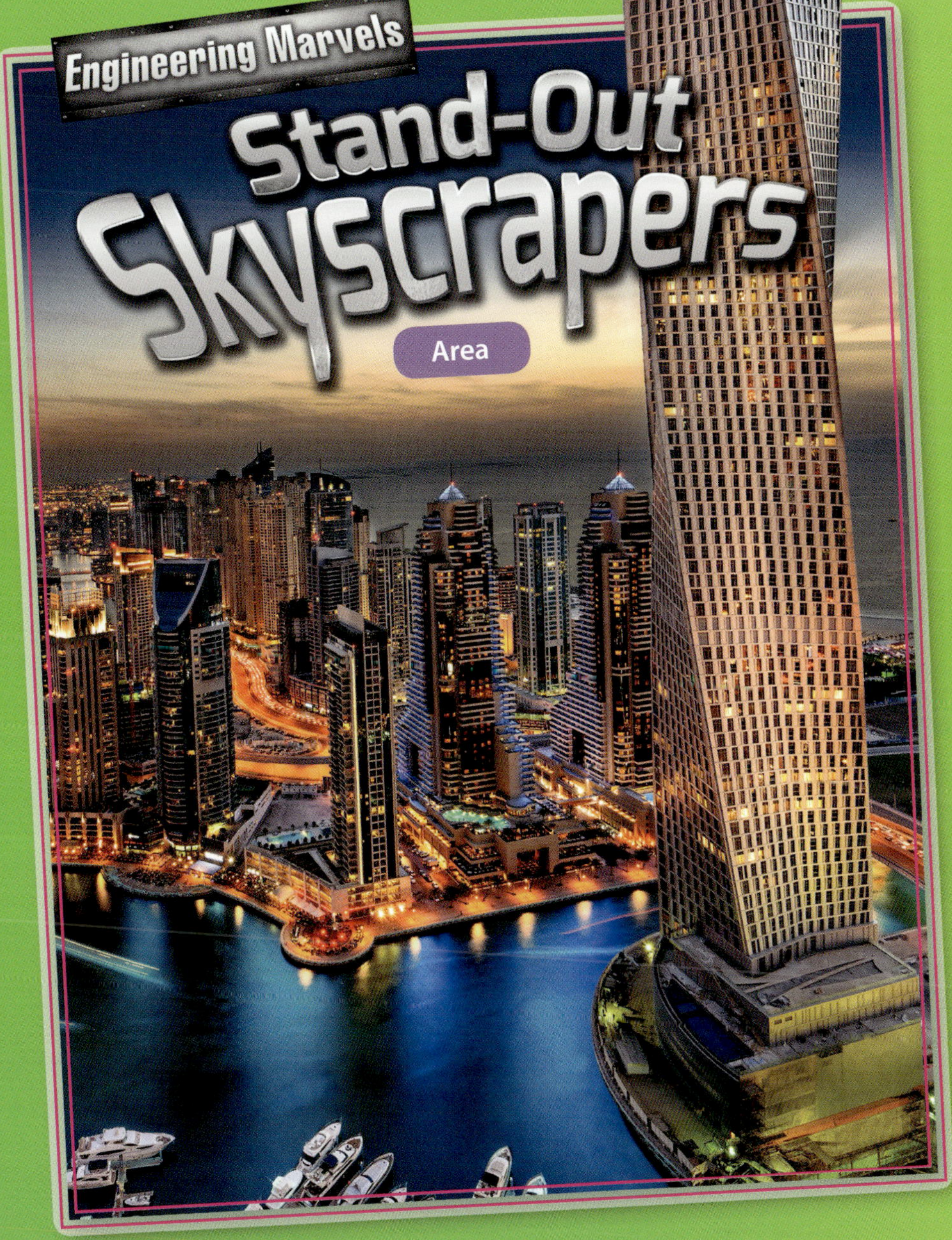

Stacy Monsman, M.A.

Contributing Author

Christina Hill, M.A.

Consultants

Michele Ogden, Ed.D
Principal, Irvine Unified School District

Jennifer Robertson, M.A.Ed.
Teacher, Huntington Beach City School District

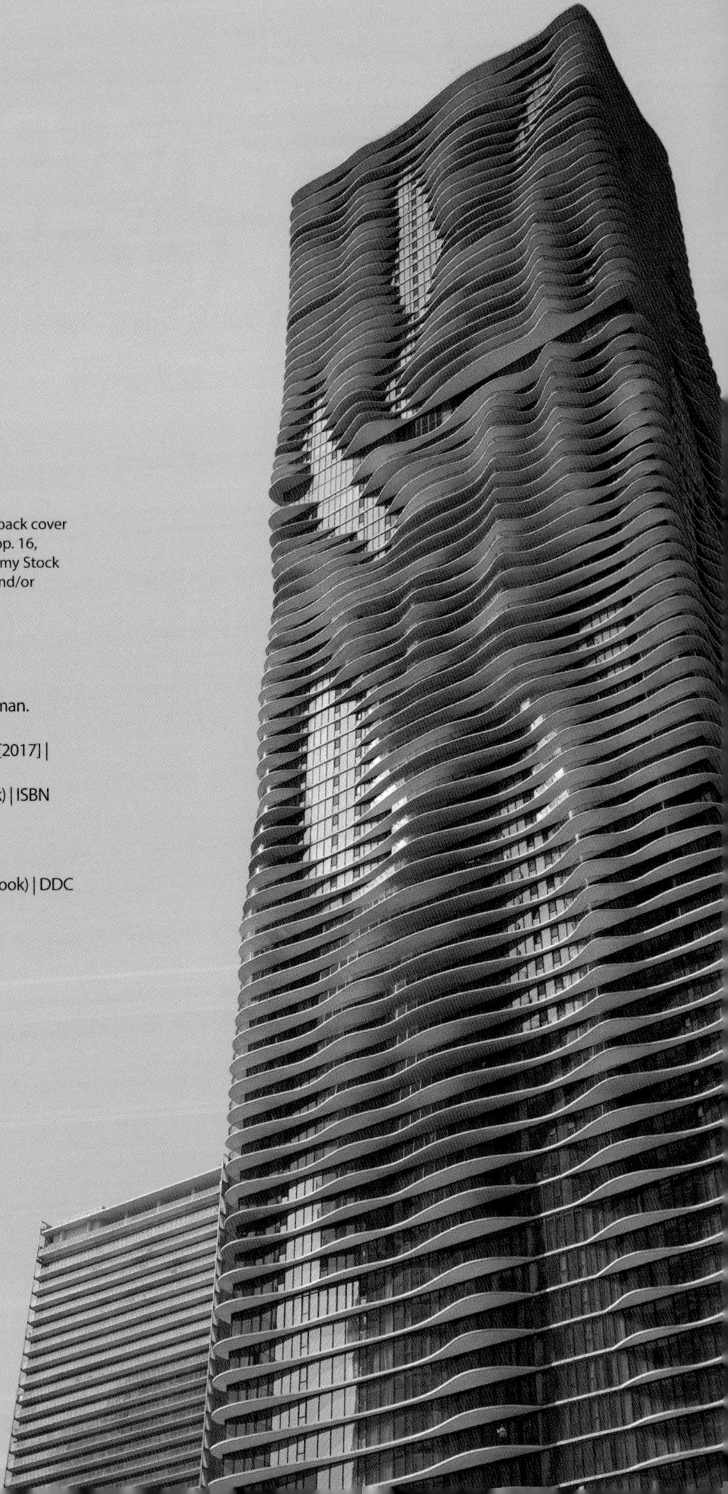

Publishing Credits

Rachelle Cracchiolo, M.S.Ed., *Publisher*
Conni Medina, M.A.Ed., *Managing Editor*
Dona Herweck Rice, *Series Developer*
Emily R. Smith, M.A.Ed., *Series Developer*
Diana Kenney, M.A.Ed., NBCT, *Content Director*
Stacy Monsman, M.A., *Editor*
Kevin Panter, *Designer*

Image Credits: p. 7 Photo courtesy of Aurelien Guichard; pp. 12 and back cover Photo courtesy of Kelly Harvey; p. 15 Jose M. Osorio/TNS/Newscom; pp. 16, 17, 18 View Pictures/UIG via Getty Images; p. 19 View Pictures Ltd/Alamy Stock Photo; p. 25 Nation Multimedia Group; all other images from iStock and/or Shutterstock.

Library of Congress Cataloging-in-Publication Data

Names: Monsman, Stacy.
Title: Engineering marvels : stand-out skyscrapers / Stacy Monsman.
Other titles: Stand-out skyscrapers
Description: Huntington Beach, CA : Teacher Created Materials, [2017] | Audience: K to grade 3. | Includes index.
Identifiers: LCCN 2016053562 (print) | LCCN 2017008590 (ebook) | ISBN 9781480758100 (pbk.) | ISBN 9781480758742 (eBook)
Subjects: LCSH: Skyscrapers--Juvenile literature. | Architecture, Modern--20th century--Juvenile literature.
Classification: LCC NA6230 .M595 2017 (print) | LCC NA6230 (ebook) | DDC 720/.483--dc23
LC record available at https://lccn.loc.gov/2016053562

Teacher Created Materials
5301 Oceanus Drive
Huntington Beach, CA 92649-1030
http://www.tcmpub.com

ISBN 978-1-4807-5810-0

Table of Contents

Towers to the Sky

"Going up!" can be heard in elevators in most buildings. Some buildings have only a few floors. But some are so high they seem to touch the sky. That is why they are called skyscrapers!

Some skyscrapers are places to live. Some are places to work. Others are places to shop. Some even have roller coasters that speed through the air. And many skyscrapers have all of these things (and more) under one roof!

Dubai

There are skyscrapers all over the world. But some skyscrapers stand out for more than just their height. They can be some of the most unusual buildings a country has to offer. From Chicago to Dubai, and cities in between, there are a few skyscrapers that are known for being unique. Which towering treasure will be your favorite?

Tip-Top Tech

All buildings need some type of technology. It helps to make them solid and support weight. It allows for a supply of energy, air, and water. But, those are basic things. Technology can be used in some exciting ways. It can make some skyscrapers even more special. And, it may also help give them a more unique look. Some were even inspired by it!

Lloyd's of London

the atrium at Lloyd's of London

Inside Out

Lloyd's of London has been in the insurance business since 1688. But, its building is much newer. Lloyd's wanted more space inside. So, the building's planners turned it inside out! Most of the stairs and elevators are on the outside. So are the air, water, and power systems. This gives more space for business.

The inside of Lloyd's is special, too. Its three main towers are topped by a 200-foot (60-meter) high **atrium**. It has a glass roof that lets in natural light. There is also a dining room from 1763! It was put in the new building one piece at a time.

Something Old, Something New

Castalia, a government building in the Netherlands, was meant to blend in with the rest of the city. But at 340 ft. (104 m) tall, it could not help but stand out!

Triangle peaks top this skyscraper's 20 floors. The rooftops are just some of the building's **distinct** features. They have helped make it a **landmark**.

LET'S EXPLORE MATH

Castalia's windows are also special. They are made of glass squares.

1. How many squares are in each row? How many squares are in each column?
2. How many squares would be needed to replace each window? Explain your thinking.
3. How many squares would be needed to replace 2 windows? How do you know?

The original Castalia was built in the 1960s. The owners wanted something newer and bigger. But, the planners did not want to knock it down. So, they built a new building around the old one. They covered the walls and the roof. Then, they placed the new triangle towers on top. Putting the old and new parts together seemed like a tough job. But, the planners had the right technology for the job. And it worked! Can you tell the old from the new?

Pants for a Giant

What size pants might a giant wear? Take a trip to China to find out! Some people think the China Central Television (CCTV) Headquarters in Beijing looks like a pair of big pants. But, the 44-story building was really made to look like a giant loop. It is meant to show that television is an endless loop of things to watch.

Since the building is in a **seismic** zone, it had to be built with earthquakes in mind. The finished building now has six sections. Visitors can make the trek up to a viewing deck. Once there, they can look out at the skyline. The bravest visitors look through three round glass plates in the floor straight down to the ground! Would you be brave enough to do the same?

LET'S EXPLORE MATH

Imagine that a wall of TVs is going to be installed for visitors in the lobby of CCTV Headquarters. There are 50 TVs. Each TV is a square, measuring 1 meter on each side. The wall is 5 meters tall and 10 meters wide.

1. What are three ways you can find the area of the wall? Will they all give you the same answer? Which is the most efficient way?
2. Will all 50 TVs fit on the wall? Will there be room for more?

Robot on the River

Thailand is a country made up of small towns. In fact, Bangkok is its only big city. Bangkok is known for its ancient palaces and temples. But these sit among new technology.

On the banks of the Chao Phraya (JOW PRY-uh) River stands a huge robot! How did it get there? One day, **architect** Sumet Jumsai saw his son's robot toy. Just like that, he was inspired, and an idea was born! That idea became this 20-story structure. This kind-looking robot reminds people that the bank it houses is modern and uses technology.

The Robot Building is fun to look at. But its parts also serve a purpose. The eyes are windows. The eyelids keep the sun out. The antennas are lightning rods. At night, the robot comes to life! Well…sort of. The eyes entertain people by "winking" along to music.

the Robot Building

Let's Explore Math

Behind the "eyes" of the robot are a dining room and a meeting room. Imagine that these are their floor plans.

1. Find the area of the imagined dining room using at least two **strategies**. Which strategy is more efficient?
2. Find the area of the imagined meeting room using at least two strategies. Which strategy is more efficient?
3. Which room has a greater area?

The Natural Look

Skyscrapers are often in cities. But, these next buildings take their cues from nature. They also boast **eco-friendly** designs.

Making Waves

Aqua Tower in Chicago has a water theme. The balconies are meant to look like waves. But, they also serve a purpose. They try to **buffer** the loud winds of the city. That way, neighbors can stand on their balconies and talk to each other without having to yell.

Aqua Tower

Aqua Tower is eco-friendly, too. It has a way to collect and reuse rainwater. And the glass windows are **heat resistant.** They make it so the building uses less energy to cool down.

Today, Aqua Tower is the tallest building in the world designed by a woman. Jeanne Gang led the team who planned Aqua Tower. They built shops, offices, and apartments. At the top is an outdoor space. It has gardens and a track. And Aqua Tower wouldn't be complete without its pool and hot tub.

Jeanne Gang

LET'S EXPLORE MATH

Imagine that an Aqua Tower visitor is inspired to put water-patterned rectangular rugs in her home. Rug 1 has a wave pattern and an area of 81 square feet. Rug 2 has a raindrop pattern and an area of 100 square feet.

1. The floor of her room is 9 feet long by 10 feet wide. How many square feet will she need to completely cover the floor of the room? How do you know?
2. Which rug should she choose? Why?

Sideways Skyscraper

China is home to many super skyscrapers. But one is not famous for its height. It is a horizontal skyscraper! The Vanke Center is in Shenzhen, China. Its towers do not stand upright. Instead, they are turned on their sides.

There are offices, apartments, and a hotel inside. The sideways towers are propped up on eight legs. They look like they are floating! At night, lights make the underside of the building glow.

Vanke Center

The building hovers above landscaped areas. This green space is open to the public. It provides open space and shade for people to rest. The gardens have tropical **vegetation**. There are native grasses, shrubs, and jasmine. There is also a farm area. The food that is grown is eaten at the Vanke Center. All of this plant life is kept healthy by rainwater. The water is filtered on the roof of the building and used for the green spaces.

LET'S EXPLORE MATH

Some of the landscaped areas at Vanke Center have unusual shapes. Imagine that this is a plan for one of the green spaces. How many square units of grass sod would need to be purchased for this imagined space?

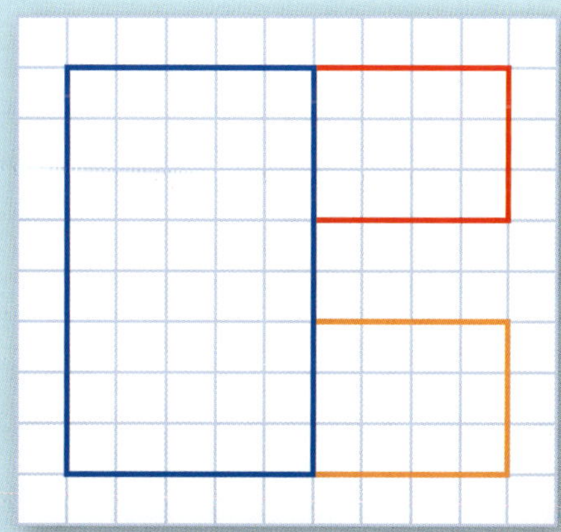

1. What is the area of each rectangle in square units?
2. Using the areas of the rectangles, calculate the total area of the imagined green space.
3. Are there different rectangles that could be used to find the area of the space?

Green and Clean

Commerzbank Tower soars about 850 ft. (260 m) over Frankfurt, Germany. That makes it the tallest building in Europe. It is also one of the greenest! It was designed a bit like a flower. The offices are the "petals." They surround a large atrium, which is the "stem." The atrium has sky gardens to help keep the air fresh.

The whole building uses natural **ventilation**. All of the windows can open to let in fresh air and light. So, the building does not use as much power. People rarely need to run the heat or turn on a fan. In fact, the building uses half the power of other skyscrapers. And, only **biodegradable** products are used to clean. They do not harm nature. There is no question as to why the tower was given the Green Building Frankfurt award.

the view inside Commerzbank Tower

a garden space at Commerzbank Tower

Aldar Headquarters

Animal Power

In homes, the wild, or zoos, animals are a big part of the world. They are a big part of some skyscrapers, too.

Happy as a Clam

Rising 360 ft. (110 m) above a beach in Abu Dhabi is the Aldar Headquarters building. It was the world's first skyscraper shaped like a circle. The unique building has diagonal grids of steel that hold it up. Looking at the building closely, you'll notice it is made of two circles. A thin strip connects the two sides. Some people think it looks like a big plate. But, it was actually inspired by a clamshell.

Building a huge circle was tough. But, the architects had technology on their side. They made 3-D models in each phase. This helped them solve likely problems. It also helped them make sure they were on track to form a perfect circle.

Drawings like this helped the architects form a perfect circle.

Climbing Koalas

In Australia, you might find koalas in eucalyptus trees. They live in them, eat the leaves, and sit on the branches. One thing koalas usually do not do is climb the sides of buildings. But, it looks like some koalas are doing just that at the Lippo Centre in Hong Kong!

The two towers are shaped like octagons. Groups of windows jut out from the rest of the building. Some people think the windows look like big letter Cs. Others see koalas grasping tree trunks!

Regardless of what the windows look like, there is plenty to see! People at the back of the building have a view of the sea. People at the front have a view of a spacious park. Inside, people are kept busy in offices, a bank, and even a bookstore.

Let's Explore Math

Businesspeople can rent office space in the Lippo Centre. If a rectangular office with a garden view has an area of 80 square feet, what are possible lengths and widths of the office?

Lippo Centre

Enormous Elephant

There is an old saying that "an elephant never forgets." And visitors to Thailand will never forget that the elephant is the national animal. Elephants are on shirts, mugs, and pens. But just in case they do forget, a skyscraper is there to remind them.

Elephant Tower

Sumet Jumsai

Sumet Jumsai built the Elephant Tower. That's right! He is the same architect who made the Robot Building! Jumsai and his team used three blocks to form the "body." They made its "eyes" out of round windows. Then, decks became the "ears." The team even built parts that look like tusks and a tail.

The 32 floors host apartments, offices, and a mall. There is even a school inside. While this building is a wonder to behold, some people just don't like it. In fact, it was once voted one of the world's ugliest buildings!

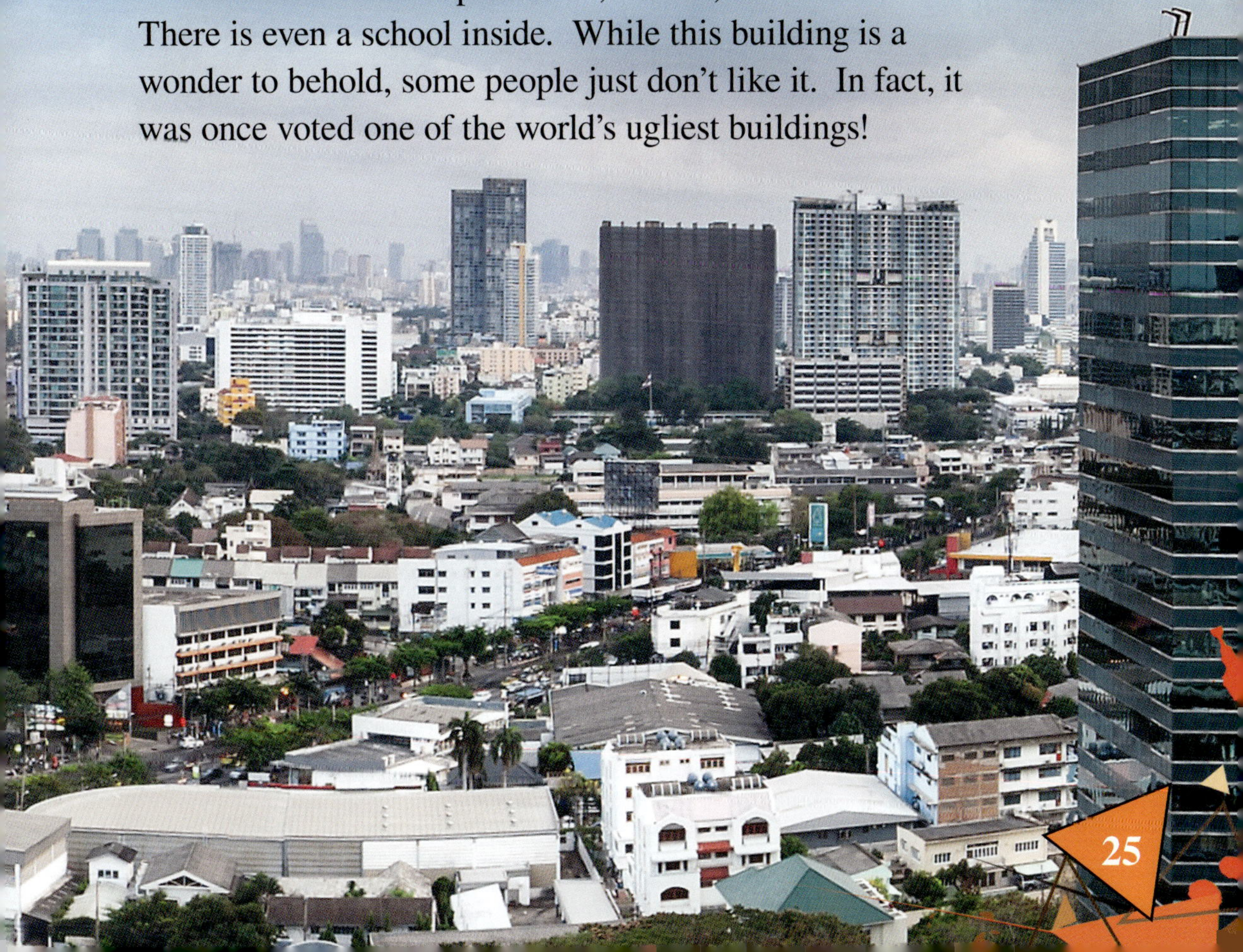

What's Next?

For many years, skyscrapers were all about height. Teams competed to build the tallest one. It seemed like they were just going to keep going up and up! As soon as one skyscraper was built, a taller one was already being planned. But, things have changed. It looks like just being tall is not enough for the newest skyscrapers.

Skyscrapers soar over London.

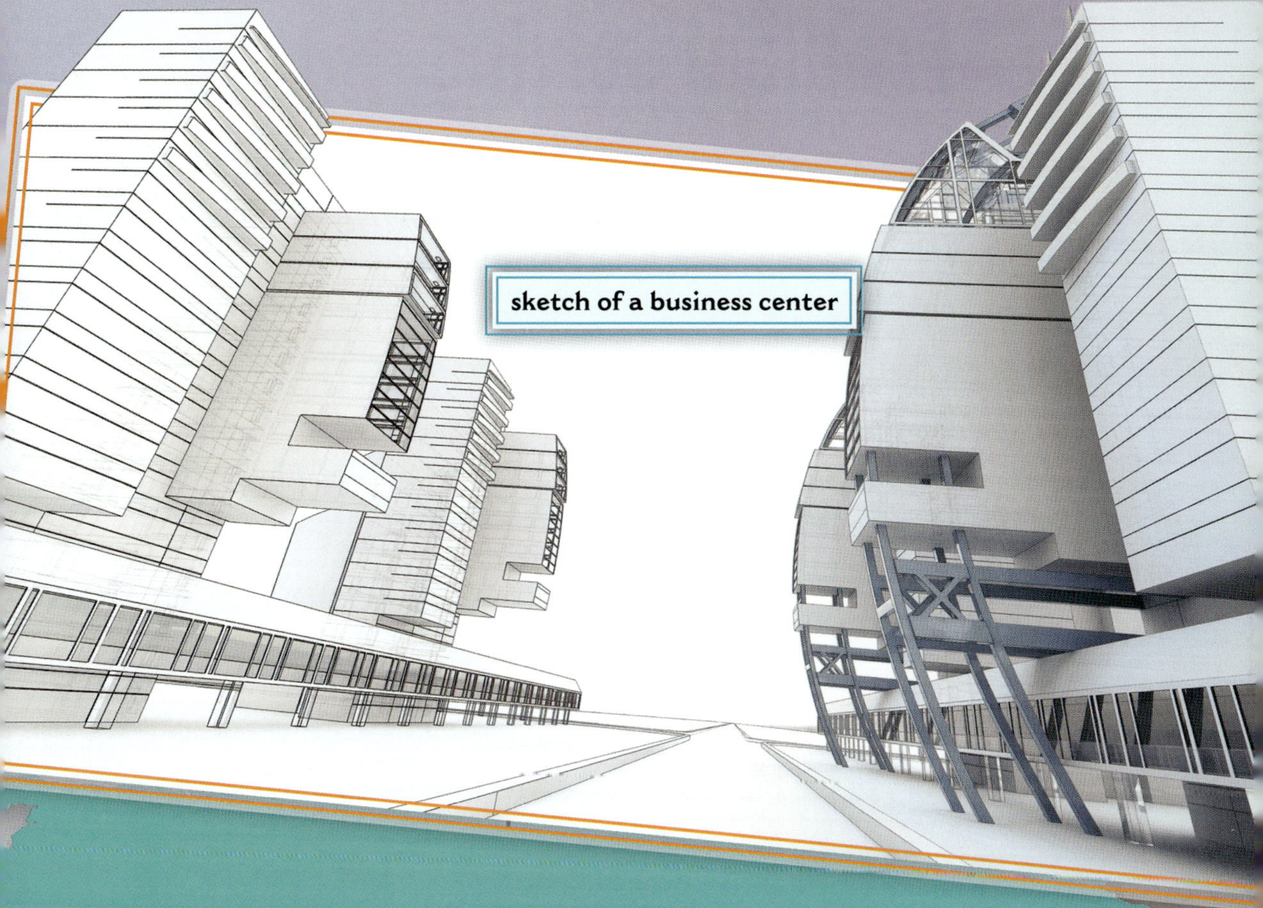

sketch of a business center

Instead, skyscrapers are getting attention for being unique. Weird shapes and special designs are what get buildings noticed. New technology is changing the way skyscrapers look. It also helps planners use space better. Buildings that are eco-friendly are also on the rise. Even animals are making their mark! In the past, architects have asked, "How high?" Now, many are asking, "What's next?"

Problem Solving

Every skyscraper you see was first planned by an architect. They start by making a **blueprint**, or floor plan. It is a detailed drawing of a building. It includes measurements of all of the rooms.

Now, it is your chance to be an architect! Your challenge is to design one floor of your own super skyscraper. What inspires you? Are you a tech pro? Maybe you are a fan of nature? Perhaps a favorite animal is going to be your inspiration. Use your imagination!

Make sure your rooms are rectangles, or shapes that can be made from rectangles. And, make sure you draw an outline of each room on graph paper. After you have drawn the floor plan for one story of the building, answer the questions.

1. How many rooms did you include?
2. Find the area of each room in square units by counting the squares.
3. Now, find the area of each room in square units using a different strategy. Explain how you know your strategy works.
4. What is the total area of your floor plan?

16,62
8,81
20,53

Glossary

architect—a person who designs buildings

atrium—an open area inside of a building that has windows which allow natural light to enter from above

biodegradable—capable of being broken down by natural processes and bacteria

blueprint—a detailed plan that shows how something will be made

buffer—to act as a protective barrier

distinct—noticeably different

eco-friendly—not harmful to the environment

heat resistant—not easily warmed

landmark—a structure or object that is easy to recognize

seismic—relating to an earthquake

strategies—careful methods for achieving particular goals

vegetation—plants that cover a specific area

ventilation—a system that allows fresh air to enter and move through a space

Index

Answer Key

Let's Explore Math

page 9:

1. 2; 3
2. 6; Strategies will vary but may include adding and skip counting.
3. 12; Strategies will vary but may include counting or tiling.

page 11:

1. Strategies will vary but may include repeated addition or multiplication. Yes; Multiplying is the most efficient because it is the fastest.
2. Yes, all the TVs will fit, but there will not be room for any more.

page 13:

1. 15 square units; Strategies will vary.
2. 18 square units; Strategies will vary.
3. Meeting room

page 15:

1. 90 sq. ft.; Strategies will vary.
2. Rug 1 because the area of Rug 2 is greater than the area of the floor.

page 17:

1. The areas of the rectangles are 40, 12, and 12 sq. units.
2. 40 + 12 + 12 = 64 sq. units
3. Yes, different rectangles can be used and the area will remain 64 sq. units.

page 23:

Possible answers: 1 ft. by 80 ft.; 2 ft. by 40 ft.; 4 ft. by 20 ft.; 5 ft. by 16 ft.; 8 ft. by 10 ft.; 10 ft. by 8 ft.; 16 ft. by 5 ft.; 20 ft. by 4 ft.; 40 ft. by 2 ft.; 80 ft. by 1 ft.

Problem Solving

1. Answers will vary. All rooms should be rectangles or composed of rectangles.
2. Answers will vary but must be in square units.
3. Strategies will vary but should include an explanation about why it works.
4. Answers will vary. Total area can be found by adding the areas of all the rooms.